**TO:** Delores

**FROM:** Love
Salley

Design by Anderson Thomas Design

Published by C.R. Gibson®
C.R. Gibson® is a registered trademark of Thomas Nelson, Inc.
Nashville, Tennessee 37214

Printed in Mexico.

ISBN 0-7667-6649-7
GB648R

# For My Friend
*Delores*

photographs by
# KIM ANDERSON

poetry by
## PAULA FINN

# I HAVE SHARED
*so much with you.*

Your listening helps me hear my thoughts,

your insight helps me understand my problems,

and your patience helps me accept my faults.

You know when I need advice,

and you know when I simply need you.

*Everything I could ever want in a friend I have in you.*

*As your friend,*

I appreciate your strengths;

I accept your weaknesses.

I do not wish to judge,

control, or change you.

*You are who you are.*

You're always there to help, to encourage,

*to remind me that I'm not alone.*

You're never too busy to be a friend.

Thank you for sharing so much of your time,

*your understanding...*

and so much of yourself.

Whenever I need to talk, you listen.

*Whenever I need to be quiet, you understand.*

Whenever I need, you give.

Your *s u p p o r t* has truly made a

difference in my self-confidence,

my happiness, and in my life.

You've forgiven my mistakes,
and helped me to forget them.

You've believed in my dreams,
and helped me to find them.

*Because of you,* I am richer –
And I will always be grateful.

*You're in my thoughts today...*

I'm thinking of you today and I'm remembering

how often you've come through for me

*when I needed you most* –

how you've always given so generously

of your time, and so freely of yourself.

I'm thinking of how easy it is

*to be with you,*

how funny things seem even funnier,

and ordinary pleasures feel special

because they are shared.

I'm *t h i n k i n g* how often
your belief in me
has made the difference
between giving up on my dreams,
and trying even harder to reach them.

I'm *r e a l i z i n g* how special you are –
and how much richer my life is
because you are in it.

So today, I'm *t h i n k i n g* of you –
of all the good things you've done,
all the kind things you've said,
and all the beautiful things you are.

# THE MORE I KNOW YOU...
*the more glad I am that I do!*

You and I . . .

understand, accept,

enjoy, support,

and care for each other.

# YOU AND I . . .

*are what friendship is all about.*

*As a friend you've taught me*

to believe in myself, to appreciate myself,

to trust myself, to accept myself.

From you, I've learned to be

a friend to myself.

Each day I discover

how important a

*f r i e n d   c a n   b e . . .*

And how lucky I am

to have one like you.

You know how to be

strong when I am weak,

comforting when I am in pain,

uplifting when I am discouraged,

giving when I am in need.

YOU KNOW HOW TO BE MY FRIEND.

*You know how to be my friend.*

The strength of our friendship

*is honesty;*

the comfort of our friendship

*is acceptance;*

the joy of our friendship

*is caring;*

the beauty of our friendship

*is us.*

*We have such good times together!*
We see the same things as funny or absurd,
and our tastes are the same in almost everything.

*We can talk for hours*
about things that are most important to us . . .
We can talk for hours about nothing at all.

*We relate as equals.*
Competition does not exist between us;
power is never important, but respect always is.

I can confide in you,

and trust you with my mistakes

and my regrets.

I can tell you things I've told

*no one else*

and I know you will never judge me . . .

or tell my secrets.

Thanks for being the friend

who's always believed in me, who's always understood,

who's always accepted me, who's always cared.

*What we have is rare...*

Let us protect it, celebrate it, cherish it . . .

LET US ALWAYS BE FRIENDS:

*Let us always be friends.*